marvellous
meat
recipes

TRIDENT PRESS
INTERNATIONAL

Published by:
TRIDENT PRESS INTERNATIONAL
801, 12th Avenue South
Suite 302
Naples, FL 34102 U.S.A.
Copyright (c)Trident Press International 2001
Tel: (941) 649 7077
Fax: (941) 649 5832
Email: tridentpress@worldnet.att.net
Website: www.trident-international.com

acknowledgements

Marvellous Meat Recipes

Compiled by: R&R Publications Marketing Pty. Ltd.
Creative Director: Paul Sims
Production Manager: Anthony Carroll
Food Photography: Warren Webb, William Meppem, Andrew Elton, Quentin Bacon,Gary Smith, Per Ericson, Paul Grater, Ray Joice, John Stewart, Ashley Mackevicius, Harm Mol, Yanto Noerianto, Andy Payne.
Food Stylists: Stephane Souvlis, Janet Lodge, Di Kirby, Wendy Berecry, Belinda Clayton, Rosemary De Santis, Carolyn Fienberg, Jacqui Hing, Michelle Gorry, Christine Sheppard, Donna Hay.
Recipe Development: Ellen Argyriou, Sheryle Eastwood, Kim Freeman, Lucy Kelly, Donna Hay, Anneka Mitchell, Penelope Peel, Jody Vassallo, Belinda Warn, Loukie Werle.
Proof Reader: Andrea Tarttelin

Includes Index
ISBN 1582791600
EAN 9781582791609

First Edition Printed June 2001
Computer Typeset in Humanist 521 & Times New Roman

Printed in Hong Kong

contents

introduction

introduction

Lean beef, lamb, pork and veal all play an important part in a balanced diet. In recent years there has been some concern about the amount of fat and cholesterol that meat contains. However, more recent studies show that as long as the meat chosen is lean and the portion size is around 125g/4oz then meat plays a valuable part in our diets. This book presents you with a range of recipes suitable for family meals and special occasions, all of which make the most of meat.

Lean beef, veal and Trim Lamb are highly nutritious foods with unique features. Low in fat, yet packed full of high quality protein and essential vitamins and minerals, lean red meat is a valuable contributor to a healthy body.

One of meat's prime nutritional benefits is as a supplier of the mineral iron. Iron is indispensable to carrying oxygen around our bodies, via our bloodstream. If you do not eat enough iron, you may become tired, have poor stamina and even become anaemic.

Lean beef, veal and Trim Lamb are some of the highest iron foods and this so called "haem iron" is the most easily used by our bodies. The haem iron in meat also helps the body maximise the iron in poorer iron ("non haem") foods such as vegetables, nuts, legumes and grains.

An average serve of lean red meat not only boosts your iron status, it easily provides up to half your daily requirements of zinc. Zinc is another mineral essential for humans, being necessary for growth and reproduction, healing and a healthy immune system.

That serving of meat is also brimming with B vitamins. Valuable thiamin, riboflavin, niacin, vitamin B6 and vitamin B12 will all be supplied in significant quantities, helping to release energy from food and maintain a healthy body.

High quality protein, essential for the building and repair of all body cells will also be provided. Meat protein is perfectly matched to your body's needs, as it contains all of the 8 essential amino acids, or protein "building blocks', needed each day.

Lean beef, veal and Trim Lamb are a unique combination of many essential nutrients in the one versatile, low fat package. They make a great tasting and nutritious contribution to any meal.

meat
purhasing guide

When purchasing meat, these tips will ensure that you purchase the best quality.

Allow 125 g/4 oz lean boneless meat per serve. Lamb and beef should be bright red in colour with a fresh appearance. Pork should be pale-fleshed with a sweet smell, not slimy or bloody. Select lean meat. If there is any fat it should be pale cream in colour.

In hot climates, take an insulated shopping bag with you to ensure meat remains cold until you get it home and refrigerate it.

Meat storage guide

The following tips will ensure that the meat you purchase stays at its best for the longest possible time.

Fresh meat should be kept as dry as possible and should not sit in its own 'drip' during storage. Store meat in the coldest part of the refrigerator. This will be the bottom shelf if your refrigerator does not have a special meat compartment.

The more cutting and preparation meat has had, the shorter the storage time - for example, mince has a shorter storage time than chops or steaks.

When storing meat in the refrigerator, place a stainless steel or plastic rack in a dish deep enough to catch any drip from the meat. Unwrap the meat and place on a rack in stacks of not more than three layers. Cover loosely with aluminium foil or waxed paper.

If your refrigerator has a special meat storage compartment, unwrap the meat, arrange in stacks of not more than three layers and cover meat loosely with aluminium foil or waxed paper.

If meat is to be used within two days of purchase, it can be left in its original wrapping. Store the package in the special meat compartment or the coldest part of the refrigerator.

Meat that has been kept in the refrigerator for two to three days will be more tender than meat cooked on the day of purchase, because the natural enzymes soften the muscle fibres.

Always store raw meat away from cooked meat or other cooked food. If your refrigerator does not have a special meat compartment, store the raw meat at the bottom of the refrigerator and the cooked meat at the top. Storing meat in this way prevents the raw meat from dripping onto the cooked meat and so lessens the likelihood of cross-contamination.

Raw and cooked meats both store well in the freezer, but as with any food to be frozen, it should be in good condition before freezing. To prepare raw meat for freezing, cut into portions required for a single occasion, such as a family meal. It is easier and more economical to take two packs out of the freezer for extra people than to cook too much through over-packing. If the meat is packed when you purchase it, remove it from the wrapping and repackage in freezer bags or suitable freezing containers.

Storage guide

Mince and sausages	2 days
Cubed beef, lamb and pork	3 days
Steaks, chops and cutlets	4 days
Roasting joints (with bone in)	3-5 days
Roasting joints (boned and rolled)	2-3 days
Corned beef and pickled pork	7 days

cooking
techniques

Cooking techniques can be divided into two groups: dry heat and moist heat methods. The moist heat methods are pot roasting, casseroling, braising, stewing and simmering. The dry heat methods are pan-frying, stir-frying, crumb-frying, grilling, barbecuing and oven roasting. The following guide will help you choose the correct cut of meat for the cooking technique you wish to use.

Pot roast

Beef: blade, brisket, chuck, round, fresh silverside, skirt, topside
Lamb: forequarter (shoulder), shank
Veal: shoulder/forequarter

Casserole

Beef: blade, brisket, chuck, round, spareribs, shin, fresh silverside, skirt, topside
Lamb: best neck, forequarter (shoulder), neck chop, shank, shoulder chop
Veal: shoulder/forequarter chop and steak, neck chop, knuckle
Pork: diced pork, leg steak

Braise

Beef: blade, brisket, chuck, round, spare-ribs, shin, fresh silverside, skirt, topside
Lamb: best neck, forequarter (shoulder), neck chop, shank, shoulder chop
Veal: shoulder/forequarter chop and steak, neck chop, knuckle
Pork: leg steak

Stew

Beef: blade, brisket, chuck, round, spareribs, shin, fresh silverside, skirt, topside
Lamb: best neck, forequarter/shoulder and neck chop, shank
Veal: forequarter/shoulder chop and steak, neck chop, knuckle
Pork: diced pork

Simmer

Beef: corned (salted) silverside, corned (salted) brisket
Pork: pickled pork

Pan-fry or Pan-cook

Beef: blade, fillet, round (minute), rump, rib eye, spareribs, sirloin/T-bone
Lamb: best neck chop and cutlet, chump, leg and mid loin chop, loin chop and cutlet
Veal: cutlet, leg steak, loin chop, schnitzel (escalope)
Pork: butterfly (valentine) steak, cutlet, fillet, forequarter (sparerib) chop and steak, leg steak, loin chop and medallion steak, schnitzel (escalope)

Stir-fry

Beef: fillet, round, rump, rib eye, topside, sirloin steak
Lamb: boneless leg, boneless shoulder, boneless mid loin, fillet
Pork: diced pork, schnitzel (escalope)

Crumb-fry

Beef: round (minute), topside steak
Lamb: best neck chop, rib loin cutlet
Veal: leg steak, schnitzel (escalope), loin chop, cutlet
Pork: schnitzel (escalope)

Grill

Beef: fillet, rump, rib eye, spareribs, sirloin/T-bone
Lamb: best neck chop and cutlet, chump,

forequarter, leg and mid loin chop, rib loin chop and cutlet, shoulder chop

Veal: leg steak, loin chop and cutlet

Pork: butterfly (valentine) steak, cutlet, fillet, forequarter (sparerib) chop and steak, leg steak, loin chop and medallion steak, schnitzel (escalope), spareribs

Barbecue

Beef: fillet, rump, rib eye, spareribs, sirloin/T-bone steak

Lamb: chump, forequarter, leg, shoulder and mid loin chop, rib loin chop and cutlet

Veal: leg steak, loin chop and cutlet

Pork: boneless loin, butterfly (valentine) steak, cutlet, fillet, loin, forequarter (sparerib) chops and steak, leg steak, loin medallion steak, spareribs

Oven roast

Beef: fillet, rump, rib roast, spareribs, sirloin, fresh silverside, topside

Lamb: breast, forequarter (shoulder), leg, mid loin, rib loin, rack, crown roast, shank

Veal: leg, loin, rack, shoulder/forequarter

Pork: fillet, loin, leg, boneless loin, schnitzel (escalope), shoulder (hand or spring), spareribs

Keeping it safe

The casual style of barbecuing can sometimes lead to casual handling of food which in turn can lead to unwelcome health problems. Follow these easy rules for safe entertaining.

Preparation

- Do not handle cooked and uncooked meat at the same time, as this encourages the transfer of bacteria from the raw to the cooked meat.
- Wash thoroughly in hot soapy water all utensils and boards that have been used for cutting raw meat, before using them to cut cooked meat.
- Remember to thoroughly wash your hands after preparing raw meat and frequently during all food preparation.
- To thaw frozen food, remove food from wrappings and place on a rack in a shallow dish. Cover loosely with plastic food wrap and place in the refrigerator to thaw. Food should be completely defrosted before cooking, this is particularly important for foods which are intended for barbecuing and for those which only have a short cooking time.
- Thawing food at room temperature, especially during the warmer months can create the ideal conditions for bacteria to multiply. If the food is then not cooked long enough or a high enough internal temperature is not reached to kill the bacteria, there is the potential for food poisoning to occur.
- Cook food as soon as possible after thawing.

pork and orange kebabs

healthy meat

Eating the right foods is essential

to your total health. It influences your vitality, your weight and your ability to fight off infections and serious illnesses. This chapter brings together which can help you and your family towards a better way of eating.

pork
and orange kebabs

Photograph page 9

Method:
1 To make marinade, place orange juice, lemon juice, garlic, tomato purée, onion, oil and honey in a bowl and mix to combine.
2 Add pork, toss to coat and set aside to marinate for 1 hour.
3 Preheat barbecue to a medium heat.
4 Thread pork, orange and red pepper (capsicum) cubes, alternately, onto lightly oiled bamboo skewers and cook on lightly oiled barbecue grill, basting frequently with marinade for 5-6 minutes each side or until pork is cooked.

Serves 4

ingredients

**500g/1 lb pork fillet, cut into
2¹/₂cm/1in cubes
2 oranges, rind and pith removed, cut
into 2¹/₂cm/1in cubes
1 red pepper (capsicum), cut into
2¹/₂cm/1in cubes**

Orange marinade
**¹/₄ cup/60mL/2fl oz orange juice
2 tablespoons lemon juice
2 cloves garlic, crushed
3 tablespoons tomato purée
1 onion, grated
1 tablespoon olive oil
2 tablespoons honey**

osso
bucco

Method:
1 Heat oil in a large frying pan and cook red peppers (capsicum) and onions over a medium heat for 10 minutes or until onions are transparent. Using a slotted spoon, remove onion mixture and set aside. Toss veal in flour and shake off excess. Add butter to frying pan and cook until butter foams. Add veal and cook for 4-5 minutes each side or until browned.
2 Stir in wine and stock and bring to the boil, stirring to lift sediment from base of pan. Boil until liquid is reduced by half. Add tomatoes and return onion mixture to pan, cover and simmer for 1 hour or until meat falls away from the bone. Season to taste with black pepper and sprinkle with parsley.

Serves 4

ingredients

**1 tablespoon olive oil
2 red peppers (capicum0, cut into
strips
2 onions, chopped
4 thick slices shin veal on the bone
¹/₂ cup/60g/2oz flour
30g/1oz butter
¹/₂ cup/125mL/4fl oz dry white wine
¹/₂ cup/125mL/4fl oz chicken stock
440g/14oz canned tomatoes,
undrained and mashed
freshly ground black pepper
1 tablespoon chopped fresh parsley**

curried
lamb soup

Method:

1 Place split peas in a bowl, cover with water and set aside to soak for 10 minutes.
2 Heat oil in a large saucepan and cook lamb shanks for 5-6 minutes or until browned on all sides. Add garlic, onion and curry powder and cook, stirring, for 5 minutes longer. Drain peas and add peas and boiling water to pan. Bring soup to the boil, skimming off any scum from the surface, then reduce heat and simmer for 1 hour.
3 Remove shanks from soup and set aside to cool. Remove meat from bones and cut into even-sized pieces. Remove peas from soup and place in a food processor or blender and process until smooth. Return pea purée and meat to pan, then stir in mint and carrots and cook for 5 minutes. Add celery, coconut milk, lemon juice and black pepper to taste and cook over a medium heat without boiling for 3-5 minutes.

Serves 4

ingredients

185g/6oz yellow split peas, washed
2 tablespoons vegetable oil
375g/12oz lamb shanks, cut in half
3 cloves garlic, crushed
1 onion, finely chopped
2 tablespoons curry powder
5 cups/1¼ litres/2pt boiling water
2 tablespoons chopped fresh mint
2 carrots, diced
2 stalks celery, sliced
½ cup/125mL/4fl oz coconut milk
1 tablespoon lemon juice
freshly ground black pepper

basil
meatball soup

Photograph page 13

ingredients

1 tablespoon olive oil
2 carrots, cut into thin strips
4 cups/1 litre/1³/₄pt beef stock
125g/4oz vermicelli
freshly ground black pepper

Basil meatballs
250g/8oz lean ground beef
1 egg, lightly beaten
3 tablespoons dried breadcrumbs
2 tablespoons grated Parmesan cheese
1 tablespoon finely chopped fresh basil
or 1 teaspoon dried basil
1 tablespoon tomato sauce
3 cloves garlic, crushed
1 onion, finely chopped

Method:

1 *To make meatballs, place ground beef, egg, breadcrumbs, Parmesan cheese, basil, tomato sauce, garlic and onion in a bowl and mix to combine. Using wet hands, roll mixture into small balls. Place meatballs on a plate lined with plastic food wrap and refrigerate for 30 minutes.*

2 *Heat oil in a large frying pan and cook meatballs for 10 minutes or until cooked through and browned on all sides. Add carrots and cook for 3 minutes longer.*

3 *Place stock in a large saucepan and bring to the boil. Add vermicelli and cook for 4-5 minutes or until vermicelli is tender. Add carrots and meatballs, season to taste with black pepper and cook for 4-5 minutes longer.*

Note: *The meatballs for this soup are also delicious made with thyme, rosemary or parsley. Or you might like to try a mixture of herbs for something different.*

Serves 4

pea
and ham soup

Photograph page 13

ingredients

15g/¹/₂oz butter
1 tablespoon olive oil
2 cloves garlic, crushed
1 onion, finely chopped
125g/4oz button mushrooms, sliced
4 cups/1 litre/1³/₄pt chicken stock
¹/₂ teaspoon paprika
3 stalks celery, chopped
10 large lettuce leaves, shredded
250g/8oz fresh or frozen peas
125g/4oz diced ham
¹/₄ red pepper (capsicum), finely chopped
2 tablespoons chopped fresh parsley
freshly ground black pepper

Method:

1 *Heat butter and oil in a large saucepan and cook garlic, onion and mushrooms for 3 minutes. Stir in stock and paprika and bring to the boil, then reduce heat and simmer for 10 minutes.*

2 *Add celery, lettuce and peas and cook for 5 minutes longer or until peas are tender. Stir in ham, red pepper (capsicum), parsley and black pepper to taste and cook for 3-4 minutes.*

Serves 4

beef
in beer

Method:

1 *Heat oil in a large nonstick frying pan and cook beef over a high heat until browned on all sides. Transfer beef to a large casserole dish.*

2 *Reduce heat to medium and cook onions and carrots for 4-5 minutes or until onions start to soften. Stir in flour and cook for 1 minute, stirring continuously, then add beer and ½ cup/125 mL/4 fl oz stock and cook for 3-4 minutes, stirring to lift any sediment from base of pan. Stir in remaining stock, garlic, ginger, honey, orange rind and black pepper to taste.*

3 *Pour stock mixture over meat, cover and cook for 1³/₄-2 hours or until meat is tender.*

Serves 4

ingredients

**2 tablespoons vegetable oil
750g/1½lb lean topside beef, cut
into 2½cm/1in cubes
2 onions, chopped
2 carrots, cut into 1cm/½in slices
2 tablespoons flour
½ cup/125mL/4fl oz beer
2 cups/500 mL/16 fl oz beef stock
2 cloves garlic, crushed
1 tablespoon grated fresh ginger
2 tablespoons honey
1 tablespoon finely grated orange rind
freshly ground black pepper**

Oven temperature 210°C/420°F/Gas 7

steak
and kidney pie

Method:

1 Place steak, kidneys and flour in a plastic food bag and shake to coat meat with flour. Shake off excess flour and set aside. Heat oil in a large frying pan and cook meat over a high heat, stirring, until brown on all sides. Reduce heat to medium, add garlic and onions and cook for 3 minutes longer. Stir in mustard, parsley, Worcestershire sauce, stock and tomato paste (purée), bring to simmering, cover and simmer, stirring occasionally, for 2¹/₂ hours or until meat is tender. Remove pan from heat and set aside to cool completely.

2 Place cooled filling in a 4 cup/1 litre/1³/₄pt capacity pie dish. On a lightly floured surface, roll out pastry to 5cm/2in larger than pie dish. Cut off a 1cm/¹/₂in strip from pastry edge. Brush rim of dish with water and press pastry strip onto rim. Brush pastry strip with water. Lift pastry top over filling and press gently to seal edges. Trim and knock back edges to make a decorative edge. Brush with milk and bake for 30 minutes or until pastry is golden and crisp.

Serves 6

ingredients

1 kg/2 lb lean topside steak, cut into
2¹/₂cm/1in cubes
6 lamb's kidneys or 1 ox kidney,
cored and roughly chopped
4 tablespoons flour
1 tablespoon vegetable oil
2 cloves garlic, crushed
2 onions, chopped
¹/₂ teaspoon dry mustard
2 tablespoons chopped fresh parsley
2 tablespoons Worcestershire sauce
1¹/₂ cups/375mL/12fl oz beef stock
2 teaspoons tomato paste (purée)
375g/12oz prepared puff pastry
2 tablespoons milk

beef
fillet wrapped in pastry

Photograph page 17

Method:

1 Melt half the butter in a large frying pan. When sizzling, add fillet and cook over a medium heat for 10 minutes, turning to brown and seal all sides. Remove meat from pan and set aside to cool completely.

2 Melt remaining butter in frying pan and cook onion for 5 minutes or until soft. Add mushrooms and cook, stirring, for 15 minutes or until mushrooms give up all their juices and these have evaporated. Season to taste with black pepper and nutmeg, stir in parsley and set aside to cool completely.

3 Roll out pastry to a length 10cm/4in longer than meat and wide enough to wrap around fillet. Spread half the mushroom mixture down centre of pastry and place fillet on top. Spread remaining mushroom mixture on top of fillet. Cut out corners of pastry. Brush pastry edges with egg. Wrap pastry around fillet like a parcel, tucking in ends. Place pastry-wrapped fillet seam side down on a lightly greased baking sheet and freeze for 10 minutes.

4 Roll out remaining pastry to 10x30cm/4x12 in length and cut into strips 1cm/¹/₂in wide. Remove fillet from freezer and brush pastry all over with egg. Arrange 5 pastry strips diagonally over pastry parcel, then arrange remaining strips diagonally in opposite direction. Brush top of strips only with egg and bake for 30 minutes for medium-rare beef. Place on a warmed serving platter and set aside to rest in a warm place for 10 minutes.

5 To make sauce, place wine in a small saucepan and cook over a medium heat until reduced by half. Add thyme, parsley and black pepper to taste. Remove pan from heat and quickly whisk in one piece of butter at a time, ensuring that each piece is completely whisked in and melted before adding the next. Whisk in cornflour mixture and cook over a medium heat, stirring until sauce thickens. Serve with sliced beef.

Serves 6

ingredients

60g/2oz butter
1 kg/2 lb fillet steak, in one piece, trimmed of all visible fat
1 onion, chopped
375g/12oz button mushrooms, finely chopped
freshly ground black pepper
pinch ground nutmeg
1 tablespoon chopped fresh parsley
500g/1 lb prepared puff pastry
1 egg, lightly beaten

Red wine sauce
1 cup/250mL/8fl oz red wine
1 teaspoon finely chopped fresh thyme or ¹/₄ teaspoon dried thyme
1 teaspoon finely chopped fresh parsley
100g/3¹/₂oz butter, cut into small pieces
2 teaspoons cornflour blended with 1 tablespoon water

Oven temperature 220°C, 425°F, Gas 7

lamb
with satay sauce

Method:

1 Preheat barbecue to a medium heat.
2 Place lamb, parsley, oregano, cumin, tomato paste (purée), onions, bread crumbs and egg whites in a large bowl and mix to combine. Divide mixture into eight portions and shape each portion into a sausage shape. Thread each sausage onto a lightly oiled bamboo skewer.
3 Cook lamb kebabs on lightly oiled barbecue grill or plate (griddle), turning frequently, for 10 minutes or until cooked through.
4 To make sauce, heat oil in a saucepan and cook garlic and onion over a medium heat for 1 minute. Stir in peanut butter, tomato paste (purée), chutney, sherry, lemon juice, coconut milk, coriander and chilli paste (sambal oelek) and cook, stirring constantly, over a low heat for 10 minutes or until sauce thickens slightly. Serve with kebabs.

Makes 8 kebabs

ingredients

750g/1 1/2 lb lean lamb mince
3 tablespoons chopped fresh parsley
1 teaspoon dried oregano
2 teaspoons ground cumin
2 tablespoons tomato paste (purée)
2 onions, grated
3/4 cup/90g/3oz dried bread crumbs
2 egg whites, lightly beaten

<u>Satay sauce</u>
1 tablespoon peanut (groundnut) oil
2 cloves garlic, crushed
1 onion, finely chopped
4 tablespoons crunchy peanut butter
1 teaspoon tomato paste (purée)
2 tablespoons sweet fruit chutney
2 tablespoons dry sherry
1 tablespoon lemon juice
4 tablespoons coconut milk
2 teaspoons ground coriander
1 teaspoon chilli paste (sambal oelek)

veal
and apricot skewers

Method:

1 *To make marinade, place yoghurt, onion, garlic, chilli paste (sambal oelek), lime juice, cumin and coriander in a food processor or blender and process to combine. Transfer to large bowl, add veal and apricots and toss to combine. Cover and marinate for 2 hours.*

2 *Preheat barbecue to a medium heat. Drain veal and apricots and reserve marinade. Thread veal and apricots, alternately, onto lightly oiled bamboo skewers and cook on lightly oiled barbecue grill, turning and basting with reserved marinade, for 10 minutes or until cooked.*

Serves 4

ingredients

**375g/12oz topside veal, cut into
2 cm/³/₄in cubes
125 g/4 oz dried apricots**

<u>**Chilli yoghurt marinade**</u>
**1¹/₂ cups/300g/9¹/₂oz natural yoghurt
1 onion, grated
2 cloves garlic, crushed
2 teaspoons chilli paste (sambal oelek)
1 tablespoon lime juice
1 teaspoon ground cumin
1 tablespoon chopped fresh coriander**

sausage
and pancetta risotto

Method:

1 Heat oil in a large frying pan, add pancetta or bacon, carrot and onion and fry for 10 minutes, stirring occasionally. Stir in tomatoes, lower heat and simmer for 15 minutes. Stir in stock and beans, remove pan from heat and set aside.

2 In a saucepan, melt butter and fry sausages with sage, rosemary and garlic for 7 minutes, stirring frequently until sausage is crumbly.

3 Add rice and wine. Stir mixture until liquid has evaporated, then add 250ml/8fl oz of bean/stock mixture. Cook until liquid has evaporated.

4 Continue adding bean/stock mixture in this fashion until all liquid has been absorbed and rice is tender, about 20 minutes. Stir in chopped pepper (capsicum) and Parmesan.

Serves 4

ingredients

2 tablespoons olive oil
90g/3oz pancetta or rindless back bacon, chopped
1 small carrot, sliced
1 onion, thinly sliced
2 x 410g/13oz cans chopped tomatoes
600ml/1pt chicken stock
185g/6oz drained canned kidney beans
30g/1oz butter
4 Italian sausages, casings removed
1/2 teaspoon dried sage
1/2 teaspoon dried rosemary
2 cloves garlic, crushed
185g/6oz Arborio rice
125ml/4fl oz red wine
1/2 red or yellow pepper (capsicum, roughly chopped
90g/3oz grated Parmesan cheese

apple
pork casserole

Method:

1 *Heat butter in a large frying pan and cook onions and pork over a medium heat for 5 minutes. Add apples, herbs, stock and black pepper to taste, bring to the boil, then reduce heat and simmer for 1 hour or until pork is tender. Using a slotted spoon remove pork and set aside.*

2 *Push liquid and solids through a sieve and return to pan with pork.*

3 *To make sauce, melt butter in a frying pan and cook apple over a medium heat for 2 minutes. Stir in chives and tomatoes and bring to the boil, reduce heat and simmer for 5 minutes. Pour into pan with pork and cook over a medium heat for 5 minutes longer. Just prior to serving, sprinkle with cracked black peppercorns.*

Serves 4

ingredients

30g/1oz butter
2 onions, chopped
500g/1 lb lean diced pork
3 large apples, peeled, cored and chopped
1 tablespoon dried mixed herbs
3 cups/750mL/1¼pt chicken stock
freshly ground black pepper

Apple sauce
30g/1oz butter
2 apples, peeled, cored and chopped
2 tablespoons snipped fresh chives
440g/14oz canned tomatoes, undrained and mashed
1 teaspoon cracked black peppercorns

moroccan
stew

Method:

1 *Heat oil in a heavy-based saucepan and cook meat over a high heat for 4-5 minutes or until browned on all sides. Stir in stock and cinnamon, bring to the boil, then reduce heat and simmer for 10 minutes, stirring to lift any sediment from base of pan.*

2 *Add honey, turmeric, nutmeg, raisins and apricots to pan, cover and simmer for 30 minutes.*

3 *Stir in onions, orange juice and almonds and simmer, uncovered, for 30 minutes longer or until meat is tender. Season to taste with black pepper.*

Serves 4

ingredients

1 tablespoon vegetable oil
500g/1 lb chuck steak, cut
into 2¹/₂cm/1in cubes
2 cups/500mL/16fl oz beef stock
2 teaspoons ground cinnamon
2 tablespoons honey
¹/₂ teaspoon ground turmeric
¹/₂ teaspoon ground nutmeg
60g/2oz raisins
60g/2oz dried apricots, chopped
8 baby onions
2 tablespoons orange juice
60g/2oz blanched almonds
freshly ground black pepper

shepherd's
pie

Method:

1 Heat oil in a frying pan over a medium heat, add onion and cook, stirring, for 2-3 minutes or until onion is tender. Stir in meat. Blend flour with a little of the stock or water to form a smooth paste. Stir flour mixture, remaining stock or water and tomatoes into pan and, stirring constantly, bring to the boil. Add peas, tomato paste (purée) and Worcestershire sauce and simmer, stirring frequently, for 5 minutes or until mixture thickens. Spoon mixture into a deep ovenproof dish or individual ramekins.

2 To make topping, place potatoes in saucepan, cover with cold water and bring to the boil. Reduce heat, cover and simmer for 15-20 minutes or until potatoes are tender. Drain well, add milk or cream and black pepper to taste and mash. Top meat mixture with potatoes, sprinkle with cheese and breadcrumbs and bake for 15-20 minutes or until top is golden.

Serves 4

ingredients

1 tablespoon olive oil
1 onion, chopped
500g/1 lb chopped cooked beef, lamb, pork or chicken
1 tablespoon flour
¹/₂ cup/125mL/4fl oz beef stock or water
440g/14oz canned tomatoes, undrained and mashed
60g/2oz frozen peas
2 tablespoons tomato paste (purée)
1 tablespoon Worcestershire sauce

Cheesy potato topping
3 potatoes, chopped
¹/₄ cup/60mL/2fl oz milk or cream (double)
freshly ground black pepper
60g/2oz grated tasty cheese (mature cheddar)
¹/₄ cup/30g/1oz dried breadcrumbs

fruity
pork roulade

Method:

1 To make filling, place pine nuts, prunes, apricots, ginger, sage, chutney, bacon, brandy and black pepper to taste in a food processor and process until finely chopped.

2 Open out steaks and pound to about 5mm/¼in thick. Spread filling over steaks and roll up tightly. Secure each roll with string.

3 Place stock, celery and onions in a large saucepan and bring to the boil. Add pork rolls, cover and simmer for 20 minutes or until pork is cooked. Transfer pork rolls to a plate, set aside to cool, then cover and refrigerate for 2-3 hours. To serve, cut each roll into slices.

Serves 6

ingredients

4 lean butterfly pork steaks
2 cups/500mL/16fl oz beef stock
4 stalks celery, chopped
2 onions, chopped

Fruit filling
60g/2oz pine nuts
100g/3¹/₂oz pitted prunes
60g/2oz dried apricots
1 tablespoon grated fresh ginger
1 teaspoon chopped fresh sage
3 tablespoons fruit chutney
4 rashers bacon, chopped
3 tablespoons brandy
freshly ground black pepper

carpaccio
with mustard mayonnaise

Method:

1 *Trim meat of all visible fat and cut into wafer-thin slices. Arrange beef slices, lettuce leaves and watercress attractively on four serving plates. Sprinkle with Parmesan cheese.*

2 *To make mayonnaise, place egg, lemon juice, garlic and mustard in a food processor or blender and process to combine. With machine running, slowly add oil and continue processing until mayonnaise thickens. Season to taste with black pepper. Spoon a little mayonnaise over salad and serve immediately.*

Note: *To achieve very thin slices of beef, wrap the fillet in plastic food wrap and place in the freezer for 15 minutes or until firm, then slice using a very sharp knife.*

Serves 4

ingredients

500g/1 lb eye fillet beef, in one piece
1 lettuce, leaves separated and washed
1 bunch/250g/8oz watercress
90g/3oz Parmesan cheese, grated

Mustard mayonnaise
1 egg
1 tablespoon lemon juice
2 cloves garlic, crushed
2 teaspoons Dijon mustard
¹/₂ cup/125mL/4fl oz olive oil
freshly ground black pepper

lamb
and spinach strudel

Method:

1 Heat 2 tablespoons oil in a large frying pan and cook onion and lamb over a high heat for 4-5 minutes or until lamb is browned. Add mushrooms and cook for 2 minutes longer. Transfer lamb mixture to a large bowl and stir in mustard, spinach, red pepper (capsicum), parsley and bread crumbs.

2 Fold filo sheets in half, brush each sheet with remaining oil and layer sheets one on top of the other. Spoon filling along the short side of pastry, leaving a 3cm/1¼in border of pastry. Shape filling into a sausage, tuck in long sides of pastry and roll up.

3 Place strudel, seam side down, on a lightly greased baking tray, brush with oil and sprinkle with sesame seeds. Bake for 40 minutes or until pastry is golden.

Serves 4

ingredients

3 tablespoons vegetable oil
1 onion, finely chopped
375g/12oz lean boneless lamb, finely chopped
185g/6oz mushrooms, finely chopped
2 tablespoons German mustard
200g/6½oz frozen spinach, excess liquid squeezed out, and chopped
1 red pepper (capsicum), finely chopped
2 tablespoons chopped fresh parsley
½ cup/30g/1oz bread crumbs, made from stale bread
6 sheets filo pastry
1 tablespoon sesame seeds

Oven temperature 180°C, 350°F, Gas 4

Oven temperature 210°C/420°F/Gas 7

oriental
spareribs

Method:

1 To make marinade, place hoisin sauce, tomato sauce, soy sauce, honey, garlic, ginger, chilli sauce and five spice powder in a bowl and mix to combine. Add ribs and toss to coat. Cover and refrigerate for 8 hours or overnight.

2 Remove ribs from marinade and reserve marinade. Place ribs in a single layer on a rack set over a baking dish. Bake, basting occasionally with reserved marinade, for 40 minutes or until ribs are tender.

Serves 8

ingredients

1 kg/2 lb pork spareribs, trimmed of all visible fat and cut in 15cm/6in lengths

Oriental marinade
¹/₄ cup/60mL/2 fl oz hoisin sauce
¹/₄ cup/60 mL/2 fl oz tomato sauce
2 tablespoons soy sauce
¹/₄ cup/90g/3oz honey
2 cloves garlic, crushed
2 teaspoons grated fresh ginger
1 teaspoon chilli sauce
1 teaspoon Chinese five spice powder

27

boiled beef dinner

country kitchen

In recipes from a Country Kitchen,

the cook will discover just how easy it is to make flaky pies and pastries, nourishing soups and slowly cooked meals to warm the heart and feed hungry families.

pork
with sauerkraut

Method:

1 Melt butter in a large saucepan and cook pork slices over a medium heat for 3-4 minutes each side, or until meat just changes colour. Remove from pan and set aside.

2 Add onions and apples to pan and cook for 4-5 minutes or until onions soften. Stir in paprika and caraway seeds and cook over a medium heat for 1 minute. Season to taste with black pepper.

3 Combine stock, wine and tomato paste. Pour into pan and cook over a medium heat, stirring constantly to lift sediment from base of pan. Bring to the boil, then reduce heat and simmer for 10 minutes.

4 Return meat to pan, stir in sauerkraut and cook for 2-3 minutes. Remove pan from heat, stir in sour cream and serve immediately.

Serves 6

ingredients

30g/1oz butter
750g/1½lb pork fillets, sliced
2 onions, sliced
2 green apples, cored, peeled and sliced
2 teaspoons ground paprika
1 teaspoon caraway seeds
freshly ground black pepper
¾ cup/185mL chicken stock
3 tablespoons dry white wine
2 tablespoons tomato paste
440g/14oz canned or bottled sauerkraut, drained
½ cup/125g sour cream

boiled
beef dinner

Photograph page 29

Method:

1 Place meat in a large heavy-based saucepan. Add brown sugar, vinegar, mint, onion, peppercorns and enough water to cover meat. Bring to the boil, then reduce heat and simmer for 1¼-1½ hours.

2 Add carrots, onions and parsnips to pan and cook over a low heat for 40 minutes longer or until vegetables are tender.

3 To make glaze, place redcurrant jelly, orange juice and Grand Marnier in a small saucepan and cook over a low heat, stirring occasionally, until well blended. Transfer meat to a serving plate and brush with redcurrant mixture. Slice meat and serve with vegetables and any remaining redcurrant mixture.

Cook's tip: To make horseradish cream, whip ½ cup/125mL cream until soft peaks form then fold through 3 tablespoons horseradish relish.

Note: Simple and satisfying, this Boiled Beef Dinner is served with creamy mashed potatoes and horseradish cream. There are sure to be requests for second helpings.

Serves 6

ingredients

1½kg/3lb corned silverside
2 tablespoons brown sugar
1 tablespoon cider vinegar
2 sprigs fresh mint
1 onion, peeled and studded
with 4 whole cloves
6 peppercorns
6 small carrots, peeled
6 small onions, peeled
3 parsnips, peeled and halved

Redcurrant glaze
½ cup/155g redcurrant jelly
2 tablespoons orange juice
1 tablespoon Grand Marnier Liqueur

potato
bacon chowder

Method:

1 Place bacon in a large, heavy-based saucepan and cook over a medium heat for 5 minutes or until golden and crisp. Remove from pan and drain on absorbent kitchen paper.

2 Melt butter in pan and cook onions, celery and thyme over a low heat for 4-5 minutes or until onion is soft.

3 Return bacon to pan, then stir in flour and cook for 1 minute. Remove pan from heat and gradually blend in stock. Bring to the boil, then reduce heat. Add potatoes and cook for 10 minutes or until potatoes are tender.

4 Remove pan from heat and stir in sour cream and parsley. Return to heat and cook without boiling, stirring constantly, for 1-2 minutes. Ladle soup into bowls, sprinkle with chives and serve immediately.

Serves 6

ingredients

250g/8oz bacon, chopped
30g/1oz butter
2 large onions, chopped
4 stalks celery, chopped
2 teaspoons dried thyme
2 tablespoons plain flour
6 cups/1 ¹/₂ litres chicken stock
2 large potatoes, peeled and cubed
300g/10oz sour cream
3 tablespoons chopped fresh parsley
2 tablespoons snipped fresh chives

old
english pork pie

Oven temperature 250°C, 475°C, Gas 9

Method:

1 To make pastry, place flour and salt in a large mixing bowl and make a well in the centre.

2 Place lard and water in a saucepan and cook over a medium heat until lard melts and mixture boils. Pour boiling liquid into flour and mix to form a firm dough. Turn pastry onto a floured surface and knead lightly until smooth. Cover and set aside to stand for 10 minutes.

3 Lightly knead two-thirds of pastry. Roll out to line base and sides of a greased deep 20cm /8in springform pan and bake for 15 minutes. Remove from oven and set aside to cool.

4 To make filling, combine pork, sage and black pepper to taste. Pack mixture firmly into pastry case and brush edges with a little of the egg yolk mixture.

5 Knead remaining pastry, then roll out to a circle large enough to cover pie. Place pastry over filling, trim pastry and press top to pastry case. Cut a 2¹/₂cm/1in circle from centre of pastry. Brush pastry with remaining egg yolk mixture and bake for 30 minutes. Reduce temperature to 160°C/325°F/Gas 3 and bake for 1¹/₂ hours. Using a spoon, remove any juices that appear in the hole during cooking. Remove from oven and set aside to cool in pan for 2 hours. Place chicken consomme in a saucepan and cook over a low heat until melted. Set aside to cool slightly, then gradually pour into pie through hole in the top. Allow to cool. Refrigerate pie overnight.

Note: Probably the most famous English pie, the pork pie dates back to the fourteenth century when it included raisins and currants. This pie is sure to be popular and is delicious as a picnic food.

Serves 8

ingredients

Pastry
3 cups/375g plain flour, sifted
1 teaspoon salt
125g/4oz lard
1 cup/250mL water
1 egg yolk, lightly beaten with
1 tablespoon water

Filling
1¹/₂ kg/3lb lean boneless pork,
cut into 5mm/2in cubes
¹/₂ teaspoon ground sage
freshly ground black pepper
2 cups/500mL chicken consomme

pea
and salami soup

Method:

1 Place split peas and water in a large, heavy-based saucepan and set aside to stand overnight.

2 Add bacon bones to pan with peas. Bring to the boil, then reduce heat and simmer for 2 hours or until soup thickens.

3 Stir in onion, celery leaves and celery and cook over a low heat for 20 minutes longer.

4 Remove bacon bones from soup and discard. Add salami and cook until heated through. Season to taste with black pepper.

5 Ladle soup into serving bowls.

Note: Variations of this soup have been around since the Middle Ages. This one with salami is perfect for a fireside supper.

Serves 6

ingredients

3 cups/750g dried split peas, rinsed
16 cups/4 litres water
500g/1lb bacon bones
4 onions, finely chopped
4 tablespoons chopped celery leaves
4 stalks celery, chopped
250g/8oz salami, cut into 1cm/¹/₂ in cubes
freshly ground black pepper

beef
and mushroom pie

Photograph page 35

ingredients

Puff pastry
90g/3oz butter, softened
90g/3oz lard, softened
2 cups/250g plain flour
¹/₂ cup/125mL cold water

Beef and mushroom filling
I kg/2lb lean beef, cut into 2¹/₂cm/Iin cubes
¹/₂ cup/60g seasoned flour
60g/3oz butter
3 tablespoons olive oil
2 onions, chopped
2 cloves garlic, crushed
250g/8oz button mushrooms, sliced
¹/₂ cup/125mL red wine
¹/₂ cup/125mL beef stock
I bay leaf
2 tablespoons finely chopped fresh parsley
I tablespoon Worcestershire sauce
freshly ground black pepper
I tablespoon cornflour blended with
2 tablespoons water
I egg, lightly beaten

Method:

1 *To make filling, toss meat in flour to coat. Shake off excess flour. Melt butter and oil in a large heavy-based saucepan and cook meat in batches for 3-4 minutes or until browned on all sides. Remove meat from pan and set aside.*

2 *Add onions and garlic to pan and cook over a medium heat for 3-4 minutes or until onion softens. Stir in mushrooms and cook for 2 minutes longer. Combine wine and stock, pour into pan and cook for 4-5 minutes, stirring constantly to lift sediment from base of pan. Bring to the boil, then reduce heat. Return meat to pan with bay leaf, parsley, Worcestershire sauce and black pepper to taste. Cover and simmer for I¹/₂ hours or until meat is tender. Stir in cornflour mixture and cook, stirring, until mixture thickens. Remove pan from heat and set aside to cool.*

3 *To make pastry, place butter and lard in a bowl and mix until well combined. Cover and refrigerate until firm. Place flour in a large mixing bowl. Cut one-quarter of butter mixture into small pieces and rub into flour using fingertips until mixture resembles coarse bread crumbs. Mix in enough water to form a firm dough.*

4 *Turn pastry onto a floured surface and knead lightly. Roll pastry out to a 15x25cm/6x10in rectangle. Cut another one-quarter of butter mixture into small pieces and place over top two-thirds of pastry. Fold the bottom third of pastry up and top third of pastry down to give three even layers. Half turn pastry to have open end facing you and roll out to a rectangle as before. Repeat folding and rolling twice. Cover pastry and refrigerate for I hour.*

5 *Place cooled filling in a 4 cup/I litre oval pie dish. On a lightly floured surface, roll out pastry 4cm/I¹/₂in larger than pie dish. Cut off a Icm/¹/₂in strip from pastry edge. Brush rim of* dish with water and press pastry strip onto rim. Brush pastry strip with water. Lift pastry top over filling and press gently to seal edges. Trim and knock back edges to make a decorative edge. Brush with egg and bake for 30 minutes or until pastry is golden and crisp.

Note: *Homemade puff pastry takes a little time to make but the result is well worth it.*

Serves 4

cornish
pasties

Oven temperature 220°C, 440°C, Gas 7

ingredients

Pastry
60g/2oz butter, softened
60g/2oz lard, softened
2 cups/250g plain flour, sifted
4 tablespoons cold water
I egg, lightly beaten

Filling
250g/8oz lean ground beef
I small onion, grated
I potato, peeled and grated
¹/₂ small turnip, peeled and grated
2 tablespoons finely chopped fresh parsley
I tablespoon Worcestershire sauce
freshly ground black pepper

Method:

1 To make pastry, place butter and lard in a bowl and mix well to combine. Refrigerate until firm. Place flour in a large mixing bowl. Chop butter mixture into small pieces and rub in flour using fingertips until mixture resembles coarse bread crumbs. Mix in enough water to form a soft dough. Turn pastry onto a floured surface and knead lightly. Cover and refrigerate for 30 minutes.

2 To make filling, place meat, onion, potato, turnip, parsley, Worcestershire sauce and black pepper to taste in a bowl and mix well to combine.

3 Roll out pastry on a lightly floured surface and using an upturned saucer as a guide cut out six 15cm rounds. Divide filling between pastry rounds. Brush edges with water and fold the pastry rounds in half upwards to enclose filling.

4 Press edges together well to seal, then flute between finger and thumb. Place pasties on a well greased oven tray. Brush with egg and bake for 15 minutes. Reduce temperature to 160°C/330°F/Gas 3 and bake for 20 minutes or until golden.

Note: Originally the portable lunch of the Cornish working man, these pasties are great eaten hot, warm or cold and are ideal for a picnic or lunch box.

Makes 6

lamb
pot roast

Method:

1 Melt 30g/1oz butter in a large heavy-based saucepan and cook meat on all sides until well browned.

2 Combine tomatoes, red wine, tomato paste, Worcestershire sauce, herbs, sugar and black pepper to taste. Pour over meat, bring to the boil, then reduce heat, cover, and simmer for 1½ hours or until meat is tender.

3 About 30 minutes before meat finishes cooking, heat oil and remaining butter in a large heavy-based frypan. Add carrots, turnips, onions and potatoes and cook until vegetables are lightly browned. Reduce heat to low and cook gently for 15-20 minutes or until vegetables are tender.

4 Remove meat from pan, place on a serving platter and set aside to keep warm. Bring sauce that remains in pan to the boil and cook for 10 minutes or until sauce reduces and thickens slightly. Serve sauce with meat and vegetables.

Cook's tip: A nut of veal, a whole chicken or a piece of topside beef are also delicious cooked in this way.

Note: Pot roasting dates back to prehistoric times when clay pots were filled with game, whole cuts of meat or poultry and vegetables then hung over a fire to simmer. Lean meats that need long slow cooking, are ideal for pot roasting.

Serves 6

ingredients

90g/3oz butter
1.5-2kg/3-4lb leg of lamb
440g/14oz canned tomatoes,
mashed and undrained
½ cup/125mL red wine
2 tablespoons tomato paste
1 tablespoon Worcestershire sauce
¼ teaspoon mixed dried herbs
1 teaspoon sugar
freshly ground black pepper
olive oil
3 carrots, peeled and halved lengthwise
3 turnips, peeled and halved lengthwise
6 small onions, peeled
3 large potatoes, peeled and halved

lamb
and vegetable hotpot

Method:

1 *Toss meat in flour. Heat butter and 1 tablespoon oil in a large heavy-based saucepan and cook meat in batches until brown on all sides. Remove from pan and set aside.*

2 *Heat remaining oil in pan and cook onions and potatoes until brown on all sides. Remove from pan and set aside. Add garlic, celery, red pepper (capsicum) and bacon and cook for 4-5 minutes. Return meat, onions and potatoes to pan. Mix in carrot, stock, wine, tomato paste and rosemary, bring to the boil, then reduce heat and simmer, covered, for 1 hour or until meat is tender. Stir in beans and cornflour mixture, season to taste with black pepper and cook for 10 minutes longer.*

Serves 6

ingredients

750g/1¹/₂lb leg lamb, cut in 2¹/₂cm/1in cubes
2 tablespoons seasoned flour
15g/1¹/₂oz butter
2 tablespoons oil
6 baby onions, peeled and bases left intact
6 baby new potatoes, scrubbed
2 cloves garlic, crushed
3 stalks celery, sliced
1 red pepper (capsicum), sliced
2 rashers bacon, chopped
1 carrot, sliced
1¹/₂ cups/375mL beef stock
¹/₂ cup/125mL red wine
1 tablespoon tomato paste
2 tablespoons finely chopped fresh rosemary
250g/8oz green beans, trimmed and cut
into 2¹/₂cm/1in lengths
freshly ground black pepper
1 tablespoon cornflour blended with
2 tablespoons water

individual
meat pies

Method:

1 To make filling, heat a nonstick frypan and cook meat over a medium heat, stirring constantly, for 6-8 minutes or until meat browns. Drain pan of any juices and add stock. Season to taste with black pepper.

2 Bring mixture to the boil, then reduce heat, cover and simmer, stirring occasionally, for 20 minutes. Stir in cornflour mixture, Worcestershire and soy sauces and cook, stirring constantly, until mixture boils and thickens. Set aside to cool.

3 Line base and sides of eight greased small metal pie dishes with shortcrust

Note: An individual homemade pie served with mashed potatoes and peas was once the traditional working man's lunch and is still a great favourite. The secret to a really good pie is a generous filling with plenty of flavour.

Makes 8 individual pies

ingredients

750g/1¹/₂lb prepared or ready-rolled shortcrust pastry, thawed
375g/12oz prepared or ready-rolled puff pastry, thawed
1 egg, lightly beaten

Beef filling
750g/1¹/₂lb lean ground beef
2 cups/500mL beef stock
freshly ground black pepper
2 tablespoons cornflour blended with
¹/₂ cup/125mL water
1 tablespoon Worcestershire sauce
1 teaspoon soy sauce

Oven temperature 220°C, 440°F, Gas 7

almond lamb pilau

cooking on a budget

It is the challenge of every home

cook to produce tasty and economical meals for the family. In this chapter you will find a collection of old favourites as well as some great new ideas that will fit the bill perfectly. Ideal for entertaining family and friends or for special family celebrations, you will never worry again about being able to afford to celebrate a special occasion.

veal
piccata

ingredients

30g/1oz flour
8 medium veal escalopes, tenderized
60g/2oz butter
125ml/4fl oz lemon juice
125ml/4fl oz dry white wine
1 lemon, thinly sliced, for garnish

Method:

1 Lightly flour the veal escalopes on both sides. Shake off excess.
2 Melt the butter in a medium frying pan over moderate heat. When the butter bubbles, add the veal escalopes and saute for about 2 minutes on each side. When the veal is almost cooked, sprinkle on the lemon juice. Using tongs or a fish slice, transfer the escalopes to a serving dish; keep hot.
3 Add the wine to the frying pan and boil over high heat, stirring constantly until the liquid is reduced to about 125ml/4fl oz. Pour the sauce over the veal.
4 Cut the lemon into paper thin slices and place 3 slices on each escalope. Serve immediately.

Serves 4

almond
lamb pilau

Photograph page 41

ingredients

2 tablespoons olive oil
1 onion, chopped
1 clove garlic, crushed
500g/1lb diced lamb
2 teaspoons curry powder
2 teaspoons ground coriander
1 teaspoon ground cumin
1 teaspoon ground ginger
1/2 teaspoon ground turmeric
2 1/2 cups/600mL/1 pt chicken stock
1 tomato, chopped
freshly ground black pepper
2 cups/440g/14oz rice
90g/3oz almonds, toasted
90g/3oz raisins

Method:

1 Heat oil in a frying pan over a medium heat, add onion and garlic and cook, stirring, for 5 minutes or until onion is tender. Add lamb and cook, stirring occasionally, for 5 minutes or until lamb is brown on all sides.
2 Add curry powder, coriander, cumin, ginger and turmeric to pan and cook, stirring constantly, for 2 minutes or until fragrant. Add 1/2cup/125mL/4fl oz stock, tomato and black pepper to taste and bring to the boil. Reduce heat, cover and simmer, stirring occasionally, for 20 minutes or until lamb is tender.
3 Add remaining stock to pan and bring to the boil. Stir in rice, reduce heat, cover and simmer for 15 minutes or until rice is cooked. Add almonds and raisins and using a fork toss to combine.

Serves 6

42

sweet
meat curry

Method:

1 Heat oil in a large saucepan over a medium heat, add onion and garlic and cook, stirring, for 3-4 minutes or until onion is tender. Add curry powder, ginger and chilli, if using, and cook, for 1 minute or until fragrant.

2 Add carrots, celery, apple, banana, sultanas, vinegar, chutney and sugar and cook for 2-3 minutes. Stir in water and black pepper to taste and bring to the boil. Reduce heat, cover and simmer for 15-20 minutes or until vegetables are tender.

3 Stir flour mixture into curry and cook, stirring constantly, for 5 minutes or until mixture boils and thickens. Stir in meat and simmer for 5-10 minutes or until heated through.

Note: Serve curry with rice and traditional Indian accompaniments such as pappadums, chutney and sambals, or boiled potatoes and steamed vegetables.

Serves 6

ingredients

2 tablespoons olive oil
1 onion, chopped
1 clove garlic, crushed
1 tablespoon curry powder
1 teaspoon ground ginger
1 teaspoon chopped fresh red chilli (optional)
2 carrots, chopped
2 stalks celery, chopped
1 apple, chopped
1 banana, sliced
2 tablespoons sultanas
2 tablespoons malt vinegar
1 tablespoon fruit chutney
2 teaspoons brown sugar
2¹/₂ cups/600mL/1pt water
freshly ground black pepper
¹/₄ cup/30g/1oz flour blended with
¹/₃ cup/90mL/3fl oz water
500g/1 lb chopped cooked beef, lamb, pork or chicken

veal
goulash

ingredients

**4x125g/4oz lean veal steaks,
cut 1cm/¹/₂in thick
1¹/₂ tablespoons paprika
2 tablespoons flour
freshly ground black pepper
1 tablespoon vegetable oil
2 onions, chopped
1 clove garlic, crushed
1 tablespoon tomato paste (purée)
3 tablespoons red wine
¹/₂ cup/125mL/4fl oz beef stock
¹/₄ cup/60g/2oz sour cream
or natural yoghurt**

Method:

1 *Trim meat of all visible fat and cut into 2cm/³/₄in cubes. Place paprika, flour and black pepper to taste in a plastic food bag, add meat and shake to coat meat evenly. Shake off excess flour.*

2 *Heat oil in a large saucepan and cook onion and garlic over a medium heat for 3-4 minutes or until onion softens. Combine tomato paste (purée), wine and stock. Stir stock mixture and meat into onion mixture. Bring to the boil, then reduce heat and simmer, covered, for 25-30 minutes or until meat is tender.*

3 *Remove from heat and stir one-third of the sour cream or yoghurt into one serving of goulash. Serve immediately.*

Serving suggestion: *Serve with fettuccine and boiled, steamed or microwaved vegetables of your choice.*

Freeze it: *Omitting sour cream or yoghurt, freeze remaining goulash in serving portions in airtight freezerproof containers or sealed freezer bags. Defrost, covered, in the refrigerator overnight. Reheat in a saucepan over a medium heat, stirring, until hot. To reheat in microwave, place in a microwave-safe dish and cook on HIGH (100%), stirring occasionally, for 2-3 minutes or until sauce boils. Add sour cream or yoghurt just prior to serving.*

Makes 4 servings

veal chops
with sun-dried tomatoes

Method:

1 Coat chops with flour. Melt butter in a frypan and cook garlic, prosciutto and rosemary over a high heat for 2 minutes. Add chops and brown on both sides.

2 Stir in wine. Bring to the boil, reduce heat and simmer for 30 minutes or until veal is cooked.

3 Remove chops and prosciutto from pan and set aside to keep warm. Increase heat, stir in tomatoes and cook until sauce is reduced by half. Stir in basil and spoon sauce over chops and top with prosciutto.

Note: Sun-dried tomatoes are becoming increasingly popular and are available from most delicatessens.

Serves 4

ingredients

8 veal chops, trimmed of all visible fat
seasoned flour
60g/2oz butter
I clove garlic, crushed
6 slices prosciutto, chopped
2 tablespoons chopped fresh rosemary
250 mL/8fl oz dry white wine
16 sun-dried tomatoes, chopped
4 tablespoons chopped fresh basil

veal
escalopes

Method:

1 Place veal slices between plastic food wrap and flatten using a mallet, until very thin. Coat veal in flour, dip in egg then coat with breadcrumbs.

2 Melt butter in a frypan until foaming. Add veal and cook for 2 minutes each side or until golden. Wrap each veal steak in a slice of prosciutto, place in a shallow baking dish and sprinkle with mozzarella and Parmesan cheeses. Spoon cream over and cook under a preheated grill for 3-4 minutes, or until cheese melts and is golden.

Note: Serve this easy veal dish with a fresh green salad.

Serves 4

ingredients

8 small, thin veal steaks
seasoned flour
1 egg, lightly beaten
185g/6oz breadcrumbs, made from
stale bread
60g/2oz butter
8 slices prosciutto
125g/4oz grated mozzarella cheese
3 tablespoons grated fresh Parmesan
cheese
125mL/4fl oz thickened cream (double)

Oven temperature 210°C/420°F/Gas 7

crunchy
family meatloaf

Method:

1 *Place beef, potato, carrot, onion, breadcrumbs, egg, tomato sauce or chutney, herbs and black pepper to taste in a bowl and mix well to combine.*

2 *Press mixture into a lightly greased 11x21cm/ 4¹/₂x8¹/₂in loaf tin and bake for 1 hour at 210°C/420°F/Gas 7 or until cooked.*

3 *Drain off excess juices and turn meatloaf onto a lightly greased baking tray. Brush with tomato sauce mixture. Combine breadcrumbs and butter, sprinkle over meatloaf and bake for 15-20 minutes longer or until topping is crisp and golden. Serve hot or cold.*

Serves 6

ingredients

750g/1¹/₂ lb ground lean beef
1 potato, grated
1 carrot, grated
1 onion, finely chopped
¹/₂ cup/30g/1oz breadcrumbs, made
from stale bread
1 egg, beaten
2 tablespoons tomato sauce or
fruit chutney
1 teaspoon dried mixed herbs
freshly ground black pepper

<u>Crunchy topping</u>
¹/₄ cup/60mL/2fl oz tomato sauce mixed
with 2 tablespoons Worcestershire
¹/₂ cup/30g/1oz breadcrumbs, made
from stale bread
60g/2oz butter, melted

daube
of beef

Method:

1 *Toss beef in flour. Shake off excess and set aside. Heat half the oil in a large frying pan over a medium heat and cook beef in batches for 3-4 minutes or until brown. Place in a casserole dish.*

2 *Heat remaining oil in same pan, add onion and garlic and cook over a medium heat, stirring, for 4-5 minutes. Add leek and cook for 2-3 minutes longer. Add vegetables to casserole dish.*

3 *Add stock, wine, herbs and black pepper to taste to pan and stirring, bring to the boil. Reduce heat and simmer until liquid reduces by half. Add stock mixture, bay leaf and orange rind, if using, to casserole dish and bake for 1¹/₂-2 hours at 210°C/420°F/Gas7 or until beef is tender.*

4 *Add zucchini (courgettes), sweet potato and parsnip and bake for extra 30 minutes or until vegetables are tender.*

Serves 4

ingredients

1 kg/2 lb chuck or blade steak,
trimmed of all visible fat and cubed
¹/₂ cup/60g/2oz seasoned flour
¹/₄ cup/60mL/2fl oz olive oil
1 onion, chopped
1 clove garlic, crushed
1 leek, sliced
2 cups/500 mL/16fl oz beef stock
1 cup/250mL/8fl oz red wine
1 teaspoon dried mixed herbs
freshly ground black pepper
1 bay leaf
few thin strips orange rind (optional)
2 zucchini (courgettes), sliced
1 large sweet potato, chopped
1 parsnip, sliced

Oven temperature 210°C/420°F/Gas 7

Oven temperature 210°C/420°F/Gas 7

family
roast

Method:

1 Place beef on a wire rack set in a flameproof roasting dish or tin. Brush beef with 1 tablespoon oil and sprinkle with black pepper to taste. Bake for 1-1¼ hours for medium rare or until cooked to your liking.

2 For vegetables, place potatoes, pumpkin or parsnips and onions in a large saucepan, cover with water and bring to the boil. Reduce heat and simmer for 3 minutes, then drain. Arrange vegetables in a baking dish and brush with ¼ cup/60mL/2fl oz oil. Bake at 210°C/420°F/Gas 7, turning once during cooking, for 45 minutes or until vegetables are tender and browned.

3 To make gravy, transfer roast to a serving platter, cover with foil and rest for 15 minutes. Stir wine or stock, mushrooms, tarragon and black pepper to taste into meat juices in roasting dish or tin and place over a medium heat. Bring to the boil, stirring to loosen sediment, then reduce heat and simmer until sauce reduces and thickens. Slice beef and serve with vegetables and gravy.

Serves 6-8

ingredients

1½ kg/3 lb piece fresh round beef
1 tablespoon olive oil
freshly ground black pepper

Roast vegetables
6 large potatoes, halved
6 pieces pumpkin or 3 parsnips, halved
6 onions, peeled
¼ cup/60mL/2fl oz olive oil

Mushroom gravy
1 cup/250mL/8fl oz red wine
or beef stock
60g/2oz button mushrooms, sliced
½ teaspoon dried tarragon

family
paella

Method:

1 *Heat oil in a large frying pan over a medium heat, add chicken and pork and cook, stirring, for 3 minutes. Using a slotted spoon, remove from pan and set aside.*

2 *Add onions, red or green pepper and salami to pan and cook, stirring, for 5 minutes or until onions are tender. Add rice and cook, stirring, for 1 minute or until rice is coated with oil.*

3 *Stir stock or water, turmeric and black pepper to taste into pan and bring to the boil. Reduce heat and simmer for 5 minutes. Add mussels and peas, cover and simmer for 5 minutes or until mussels open. Discard any mussels that do not open after 5 minutes cooking.*

4 *Return chicken and pork to pan and simmer, uncovered, for 5-10 minutes or until all the liquid is absorbed and rice is tender. Serve immediately.*

Serves 6

ingredients

1/4 cup/60mL/2fl oz olive oil
4 chicken thigh fillets or 2 boneless chicken breast fillets, sliced
250g/8oz diced lean pork
2 onions, chopped
1 small red or green pepper, sliced
60g/2oz hot Spanish salami, sliced
3 cups/660g/1 lb 5oz rice
3 cups/750mL/1 1/4pt chicken stock or water
1/2 teaspoon ground turmeric
freshly ground black pepper
500g/1 lb mussels, scrubbed, beards removed
60g/2oz frozen peas

spinach
burghul salad

Method:

1 Place bread on a baking tray and bake for 10 minutes or until crisp and golden. Set aside to cool, then store in an airtight container until needed.

2 Place cracked wheat (burghul) in a bowl, add water and lemon juice and mix to combine. Set aside to soak for 15 minutes or until all the liquid is absorbed.

3 Place spinach leaves in a salad bowl, add cracked wheat (burghul), tomatoes, onion, bacon, oil, vinegar and basil and toss to combine. Just prior to serving, scatter with croûtons.

Serves 6

ingredients

2 slices bread, crusts removed, cubed
¼ cup/45g/1½oz cracked wheat (burghul)
¼ cup/60mL/2fl oz water
2 tablespoons lemon juice
1 bunch/500g/1 lb English spinach
2 tomatoes, chopped
1 onion, sliced
3 rashers bacon, grilled and chopped
2 tablespoons olive oil
1 tablespoon cider vinegar
½ teaspoon dried basil leaves

glazed pork spare ribs

barbecue meals

Whether it's a special celebration

or just a few friends around for a bite to eat and a chat, barbecuing is a wonderful way to entertain. A barbecue can be as formal or as casual as the host chooses and the food as simple or as sophisticated as is required.

best
barbecue sausages

Method:

An enticingly wide range of sausages is available in packages or loose from butchers, food stores and delicatessens. They may be thick, thin or chipolata (cocktail sausages). Sausages require careful cooking so the outside is crispy brown and the centre cooked through, but not dry. Blanching the sausages first plumps up the meal or filler, releases some of the fat and ensures that thick sausages will be cooked through. Separate sausages by cutting between the links with a sharp knife. Place in a saucepan, cover with cold water, bring to the boil and simmer gently for 5 minutes. Drain, then pierce sausages all over with a skewer. Place sausages, in 1 layer, on an oiled rack over moderately hot coals and cook, turning constantly, for 10-15 minutes for thick sausages, 5-8 minutes for thin ones, or until cooked through and browned.

glazed
pork spare ribs

Photograph page 53

ingredients

1kg/2lb pork spare ribs (American-Style)

Soy and honey marinade
¹/₄ cup/60ml/2fl oz soy sauce
2 tablespoons honey
1 tablespoon sherry
2 cloves garlic, crushed
1 teaspoon grated fresh ginger

Method:

1 Place spare ribs on a large sheet of heavy-duty foil and cover both sides generously with marinade. Wrap into a double-folded parcel, making sure all joins are well-sealed to prevent leakage. Stand for at least half an hour before cooking. Place in refrigerator if not to be cooked immediately.

2 Prepare the barbecue for direct-heat cooking. Place a wire cake-rack on the grill bars to stand 2¹/₂cm/1in above the bars. Place ribs in the foil parcel on the rack and cook for 10 minutes each side.

3 Remove to a plate, remove ribs and discard foil, then return ribs to rack. Continue cooking brushing with fresh sauce or marinade and turning each minute until ribs are well browned and crisp (about 10 minutes). Total cooking time is approximately 30/35 minutes.

Note: Ribs may be cooked by indirect heat in a hooded barbecue. There is no need to wrap in foil. Place over indirect heat after marinating. Brush and turn frequently with lid down for 1 hour or more. Cooking in the foil over direct heat cuts cooking time in half.

Serves 4

kettle
roasted honey beef

Method:

1 To make marinade, place mustard seeds and wine in a bowl and soak for 30 minutes. Add black peppercorns, tarragon leaves, sage leaves and honey and mix to combine.

2 Place beef in a shallow dish and pour over marinade. Cover and marinate, turning occasionally, for at least 1 hour.

3 Preheat a covered barbecue to a high heat.

4 Drain beef and reserve marinade. Place beef on barbecue grill and cook, turning frequently, until brown on all sides. Remove beef from barbecue and reduce heat to medium. Line a barbecue roasting rack with bay branches and place beef on top. Strain reserved marinade and spread mustard seeds and herbs over beef. Pour marinating liquid into a roasting tin. Place rack in roasting tin, cover barbecue with lid and cook, turning occasionally for 35-55 minutes or until beef is cooked to your liking.

Serves 8

ingredients

1½ kg/3 lb piece sirloin, trimmed of excess fat
6-8 branches bay tree

Mustard wine marinade
4 tablespoons mustard seeds
1½ cups/375mL/12fl oz red wine
1 tablespoon coarsely crushed black peppercorns
1 tablespoon fresh tarragon leaves
1 tablespoon fresh sage leaves
2 tablespoons honey

sweet
rosemary cutlets

Method:

1 Make 2 slits in the thin outer fat covering of each cutlet and insert a rosemary sprig into each one. Place prepared cutlets in a shallow dish.

2 To make marinade, place wine, honey, mustard and black peppercorns to taste in a bowl and mix to combine. Pour marinade over cutlets, turn to coat and marinate for 40 minutes.

3 Preheat barbecue to a high heat. Drain cutlets, place on oiled barbecue grill and cook for 4-5 minutes each side or until cooked to your liking.

Serves 6

ingredients

**12 small double lamb cutlets
(allow 2 double cutlets per serve)
24 small sprigs rosemary**

<u>**Honey and wine marinade**</u>
**1 cup/250mL/8fl oz red wine
¹/₃ cup/90mL/3fl oz honey
2 tablespoons wholegrain mustard
crushed black peppercorns**

italian
hamburgers

Method:

1 *To make patties, place beef, sun-dried tomatoes, parsley, basil, garlic and Worcestershire sauce in a bowl and mix to combine. Shape mixture into 8 mini patties, place on a plate lined with plastic food wrap and chill until required.*

2 *Preheat barbecue to a high heat. Brush eggplant (aubergine) slices and pepper (capsicum) quarters with oil and cook on barbecue grill for 2 minutes each side or until tender. Place in a bowl, add vinegar and toss to combine.*

3 *Reduce barbecue heat to medium, then cook patties for 4 minutes each side or until cooked to your liking. To assemble, spread base of rolls with pesto, then top with some rocket leaves, a patty, some slices of eggplant (aubergine) and a piece of red pepper (capsicum) and cover with top of roll. Serve immediately.*

Makes 8 mini hamburgers

ingredients

2 small eggplant (aubergines), thinly sliced
2 red peppers (capsicum), quartered
2 tablespoons olive oil
¹/₃ cup/90mL/3fl oz balsamic vinegar
8 mini rosetta rolls, split
3 tablespoons ready-made pesto
125g/4oz rocket leaves

<u>Beef patties</u>
500g/1 lb lean ground beef
3 tablespoons finely chopped sun-dried tomatoes
2 tablespoons chopped fresh parsley
1 tablespoon chopped fresh basil
2 cloves garlic, crushed
1 tablespoon Worcestershire sauce

barbecued
port-glazed lamb

Method:

1 *Preheat covered barbecue to a medium heat.*
2 *To make glaze, place mustard, orange rind, nutmeg, port, honey and vinegar in a saucepan, bring to simmering over a low heat and simmer until mixture thickens and reduces slightly.*
3 *Place lamb on a wire rack set in a roasting tin and brush with glaze. Pour port wine and water into roasting tin, cover barbecue with lid and cook for 2 hours, brushing with glaze at 15-minute intervals, or until cooked to your liking.*

Serves 8

ingredients

2¹/₂kg/5 lb leg of lamb
1 cup/250mL/8fl oz port
1¹/₂ cups/375mL/12fl oz water

Port glaze
4 tablespoons Dijon mustard
2 teaspoons finely grated orange rind
¹/₂ teaspoon grated nutmeg
1¹/₂ cups/375mL/12fl oz port wine
¹/₂ cup/125mL/4fl oz honey
2 tablespoons balsamic vinegar

slow-roasted
leg of lamb

Method:

1 *To make marinade, place rosemary, mint, vinegar, oil and black pepper to taste in a bowl and mix to combine.*

2 *Cut several deep slits in the surface of the lamb. Fill each slit with a slice of garlic. Place lamb in a glass or ceramic dish, pour over marinade, turn to coat, cover and marinate in the refrigerator for 4 hours.*

3 *Preheat covered barbecue to a medium heat. Place lamb on a wire rack set in a roasting tin and pour over marinade. Place roasting tin on rack in barbecue, cover barbecue with lid and cook, basting occasionally, for 1½-2 hours or until lamb is tender. Cover and stand for 15 minutes before carving.*

Serves 6

ingredients

**1½kg/3 lb leg of lamb
3 cloves garlic, thinly sliced**

Fresh herb marinade
**4 tablespoons chopped fresh rosemary
4 tablespoons chopped fresh mint
½ cup/125mL/4fl oz white
wine vinegar
¼ cup/60mL/2fl oz olive oil
freshly ground black pepper**

herbed
and spiced pork loin

barbecue
meals

Method:

1 To make marinade, place onion, pink peppercorns, green peppercorns, coriander, black pepper, cumin, garam masala, mixed spice, turmeric, paprika, salt, peanut oil, sesame oil and vinegar into a food processor or blender and process to make a paste.

2 Rub marinade over pork, place in a glass or ceramic dish, cover and marinate in the refrigerator overnight.

3 Place pork on a wire rack set in a baking dish and bake for 1 hour. Preheat barbecue to a medium heat. Transfer pork to lightly oiled barbecue grill and cook, turning frequently, for 1¹/₂ hours or until pork is tender and cooked through. Stand for 10 minutes before carving and serving.

Note: This recipe can be cooked in a covered barbecue, in which case it is not necessary to precook the pork in the oven. If cooking in a covered barbecue preheat the barbecue to a medium heat and cook for 2-2¹/₂ hours. When scoring the rind take care not to cut through into the flesh.

Serves 8

ingredients

2 kg/4 lb boneless pork loin, rolled and rind scored at 2cm/³/₄in intervals

Herb and spice marinade
1 onion, chopped
2 tablespoons crushed pink peppercorns
2 tablespoons crushed green peppercorns
2 tablespoons ground coriander
1 tablespoon freshly ground black pepper
1 tablespoon ground cumin
1 teaspoon garam masala
1 teaspoon ground mixed spice
1 teaspoon turmeric
1 teaspoon paprika
1 teaspoon sea salt
2 tablespoons peanut oil
2 tablespoons sesame oil
1 tablespoon white vinegar

californian
pork kebabs

Method:

1 To make marinade, place onion, garlic, chillies, thyme, oregano, cumin, black pepper, lemon juice, pineapple juice and oil into a food processor or blender and process until smooth.

2 Place pork in a glass or ceramic bowl, pour over marinade and toss to combine. Cover and marinate at room temperature for 2 hours or in the refrigerator overnight.

3 Preheat barbecue to a medium heat. Drain pork well. Thread pork and pineapple, alternately, onto lightly oiled skewers. Place skewers on lightly oiled barbecue grill and cook, turning several times, for 5-8 minutes or until pork is tender and cooked through.

Serves 6

ingredients

**500g/1 lb pork fillets, cut
into 2cm/³/₄in cubes
1 small pineapple, cut into
2cm/³/₄in cubes**

Pineapple marinade
**1 onion, chopped
3 cloves garlic, chopped
2 dried red chillies
2 tablespoons chopped fresh thyme
2 tablespoons chopped fresh oregano
2 teaspoons ground cumin
2 teaspoons freshly ground black pepper
¹/₃ cup/90mL/3fl oz lemon juice
¹/₃ cup/90mL/3fl oz pineapple juice
2 tablespoons olive oil**

drunken
sirloin steaks

Method:

1 To make marinade, place beer, garlic, Worcestershire sauce and tomato sauce in a large shallow glass or ceramic dish and mix to combine.

2 Add steaks to marinade, turn to coat, cover and set aside to marinate at room temperature for at least 3 hours or in the refrigerator overnight. Turn occasionally during marinating.

3 Preheat barbecue to hot. Drain steaks and reserve marinade. Cook steaks on lightly oiled barbecue, brushing with reserved marinade, for 3-5 minutes each side or until cooked to your liking. Serve immediately.

Note: When testing to see if a steak is cooked to your liking, press it with a pair of blunt tongs. Do not cut the meat, as this causes the juices to escape. Rare steaks will feel springy, medium slightly springy and well-done will feel firm.

Serves 8

ingredients

8 sirloin steaks, trimmed of all visible fat

Drunken marinade
¾ cup/185mL/6fl oz beer
2 cloves garlic, crushed
¼ cup/60mL/2fl oz Worcestershire sauce
¼ cup/60mL/2fl oz tomato sauce

pork
skewers with salsa

Method:

1 Place pork, breadcrumbs, onion, garlic, oregano, cumin, chilli powder and egg in a bowl and mix to combine.
2 Shape tablespoons of pork mixture into balls, place on a plate lined with plastic food wrap, cover and refrigerate for 30 minutes.
3 Preheat barbecue to a medium heat. Thread four balls onto a lightly oiled skewer. Repeat with remaining balls. Place skewers on lightly oiled barbecue grill and cook, turning frequently, for 8 minutes or until cooked through.
4 To make salsa, heat oil in a frying pan over a medium heat, add onion and cook, stirring, for 3 minutes or until onion is golden. Add artichokes, tomatoes, tomato paste (purée) and oregano and cook, stirring, for 3-4 minutes longer or until heated through. Serve with skewers.

Serves 4

ingredients

500g/1lb lean pork mince
1 cup/60g/2oz breadcrumbs, made from stale bread
1 onion, chopped
2 cloves garlic, crushed
1 tablespoon chopped oregano
1 teaspoon ground cumin
^{1}/$_2$ teaspoon chilli powder
1 egg, lightly beaten

Artichoke salsa
1 tablespoon olive oil
1 onion, chopped
185g/6oz marinated artichoke hearts, chopped
4 tomatoes, seeded and chopped
2 tablespoons tomato paste (purée)
1 tablespoon chopped fresh oregano

Thai fried noodles

exotic
tastes

Sensational Eastern food, based on

traditional recipes and cooking techniques which reflect

a style of cuisine that appeals to the modern cook.

warm
lamb salad

ingredients

250g/8oz assorted lettuce leaves
I cucumber, sliced lengthwise
into thin strips
2 teaspoons vegetable oil
500g/I lb lamb fillets, trimmed of all
visible fat, thinly sliced

Coriander and chilli dressing
2 tablespoons chopped fresh coriander
I tablespoon brown sugar
¹/₄ cup/60mL/2fl oz soy sauce
2 tablespoons sweet chilli sauce
2 tablespoons lime juice
2 teaspoons fish sauce

Method:
1 To make dressing, place coriander, sugar, soy and chilli sauces, lime juice and fish sauce in a bowl and mix to combine. Set aside.
2 Arrange lettuce leaves and cucumber on a serving platter and set aside.
3 Heat oil in a wok over a high heat, add lamb and stir-fry for 2 minutes or until brown. Place lamb on top of lettuce leaves, drizzle with dressing and serve immediately.
Serves 4

thai
fried noodles

Photograph page 65

ingredients

vegetable oil for deep-frying
250g/8oz rice vermicelli noodles
2 teaspoons sesame oil
2 onions, chopped
2 cloves garlic, crushed
185g/6oz pork fillets, chopped
185g/6oz boneless chicken
breast fillets, chopped
I teaspoon dried chilli flakes
125g/4oz bean sprouts
2 tablespoons Thai fish sauce (nam pla)
I tablespoon lemon juice
2 teaspoons tamarind concentrate

Method:
1 Heat vegetable oil in a wok or large saucepan over a high heat until very hot. Deep-fry noodles, a few at a time, for 1-2 minutes or until lightly golden and puffed. Remove and set aside. ·
2 Heat sesame oil in a wok or frying pan over a meduim heat, add onions and garlic and stir-fry for 4 minutes or until soft and golden. Add pork, chicken and chilli flakes and stir-fry for 4 minutes or until pork and chicken are brown and cooked.
3 Add bean sprouts, fish sauce, lemon juice, tamarind and noodles and stir-fry for 2 minutes or until heated through. Serve immediately.
Serves 4

spiced
grilled beef

Method:

1 Place onion, garlic, coriander roots, peppercorns, soy sauce, lime juice and fish sauce in a food processor and process to make a paste. Coat beef with spice mixture and cook over a medium charcoal or gas barbecue, turning occasionally, for 15 minutes or until beef is cooked to medium doneness. Alternatively, bake beef in oven for 30-45 minutes or until cooked to medium doneness.

2 Arrange lettuce, tomatoes and cucumber on a serving plate. Slice beef thinly and arrange over lettuce. Serve with lime wedges.

Serves 4

ingredients

1 red onion, chopped
4 cloves garlic, crushed
2 fresh coriander roots
1 teaspoon crushed black peppercorns
2 tablespoons light soy sauce
2 teaspoons lime juice
2 teaspoons Thai fish sauce (nam pla)
500g/1 lb rib-eye (scotch fillet)
of beef, in one piece
6 lettuce leaves
185g/6oz cherry tomatoes, halved
1 cucumber, cut into strips
lime wedges

pork
spring rolls

Photograph page 69

ingredients

24 spring roll wrappers, each
12½cm/5in square
vegetable oil for deep-frying
sweet chilli sauce

<u>Pork and coriander filling</u>
2 teaspoons peanut oil
3 red or golden shallots, chopped
2 teaspoons finely grated fresh ginger
I fresh red chilli, seeded and chopped
500g/I lb ground pork meat
2 tablespoons chopped fresh
coriander leaves
2 tablespoons kechap manis

Method:

1 *To make filling, heat peanut oil in a frying pan over a high heat, add shallots, ginger and chilli and stir-fry for 2 minutes. Add pork and stir-fry for 4-5 minutes or until pork is brown. Stir in coriander and kechap manis and cook for 2 minutes longer. Remove pan from heat and set aside to cool.*

2 *To assemble, place 2 tablespoons of filling in the centre of each wrapper, fold one corner over filling, then tuck in sides, roll up and seal with a little water.*

3 *Heat vegetable oil in a wok or large saucepan until a cube of bread dropped in browns in 50 seconds and cook spring rolls, a few at a time, for 3-4 minutes or until crisp and golden. Drain on absorbent kitchen paper and serve with chilli sauce for dipping.*
   Note: *When working with spring roll and wonton wrappers place them under a damp teatowel to prevent them from drying out. Kechap manis is a thick sweet seasoning sauce. It is made from soy sauce, sugar and spices. If unavailable soy sauce or a mixture of soy sauce and dark corn syrup can be used in its place.*
   Makes 24

---

beef
curry puffs

Photograph page 69

ingredients

625g/I¼ lb prepared puff pastry
vegetable oil for deep-frying
sweet chilli sauce

<u>Spicy beef filling</u>
2 teaspoons vegetable oil
4 red or golden shallots, chopped
I tablespoon mild curry paste
2 teaspoons ground cumin
500g/I lb lean ground beef
2 tablespoons chopped fresh coriander leaves

Method:

1 *To make filling, heat oil in a frying pan over a high heat, add shallots, curry paste and cumin and stir-fry for 2 minutes. Add beef and stir-fry for 5 minutes or until brown. Remove pan from heat and stir in coriander. Set aside to cool.*

2 *Roll out pastry to 3mm/⅛in thick and cut into 10cm/4in squares. With one point of the pastry square facing you, place 2-3 tablespoons of filling in the centre and lightly brush edges with water, then fold over point to meet the one opposite. Press together and roll edges to form a crescent-shaped parcel. Repeat with remaining pastry and filling.*

3 *Heat vegetable oil in a large saucepan until a cube of bread dropped in browns in 50 seconds and cook puffs, a few at a time, for 2 minutes or until puffed and golden. Drain on absorbent kitchen paper and serve with chilli sauce for dipping.*
   Makes 24

exotic
tastes

thai
fried rice

Photograph page 71

Method:
1 *Heat oil in a large frying pan. Add garlic and pork and fry until pork is golden brown.*
2 *Add capsicum (pepper), spring onions, fish sauce, tomato sauce, prawns (shrimp) and rice, cook over a moderate heat for 3 minutes.*
3 *Stir in beaten eggs and mix lightly through. Cover with a lid and cook for 2-3 minutes, stirring once or twice*
Note: *This fried rice is great when entertaining a crowd. It serves 8 as a main meal or 10-12 with other dishes at a party. The recipe is easily doubled or halved.*
Serves 8

ingredients

2 tablespoons oil
4 cloves garlic, crushed
400g/13oz lean pork, chopped
2 red or green capsicums (peppers), chopped
4 spring onions, chopped
4 tablespoons fish sauce
4 tablespoons tomato sauce
375g/12oz cooked prawns (shrimp), peeled
8 cups/1¹/₂kg/3lb cooked long-grain rice
2 eggs, lightly beaten

minted
pork and mango salad

Method:
1 *Heat oil in a wok over a medium heat, add pork, water chestnuts and lemon grass and stir-fry for 5 minutes or until pork is brown. Remove from wok and set aside to cool.*
2 *Place pork mixture, lime juice and fish sauce in a bowl and mix to combine. Add bean sprouts, spring onions, mint, coriander and black pepper to taste and toss gently.*
3 *Line a serving platter with lettuce leaves, then top with mangoes and pork mixture. Scatter with hazelnuts.*
Note: *This salad can be prepared to the end of step 2 several hours in advance. Cover and keep at room temperature.*
If preparing more than 2 hours in advance store in the refrigerator and remove 30 minutes before you are ready to assemble and serve it.
Serves 4

ingredients

1 tablespoon vegetable oil
500g/1 lb lean ground pork meat
60g/2oz canned water chestnuts, chopped
2 stalks fresh lemon grass, finely chopped or 1 teaspoon dried lemon grass, soaked in hot water until soft
2 tablespoons lime juice
1 tablespoon fish sauce
60g/2oz bean sprouts
3 spring onions, chopped
4 tablespoons chopped fresh mint
2 tablespoons chopped fresh coriander
freshly ground black pepper
250g/8oz assorted lettuce leaves
2 mangoes, peeled and sliced
60g/2oz hazelnuts, roasted and chopped

chilli
beef

exotic
tastes

Method:

1 *Place beef, garlic, ginger and curry paste in a bowl and mix to combine.*

2 *Heat sesame and vegetable oils together in a wok over a high heat, add beef mixture and stir-fry for 5 minutes or until beef is brown. Remove beef mixture from pan and set aside.*

3 *Add onion to pan and stir-fry over a medium heat for 3 minutes or until golden. Add green capsicum (pepper), red capsicum (pepper), sweet corn and bamboo shoots and stir-fry for 5 minutes longer or until vegetables are tender.*

4 *Return beef to pan, stir in fish sauce, sugar and stock and bring to simmering. Simmer, stirring occasionally, for 10 minutes or until beef is tender.*

Note: *When handling fresh chillies, do not put your hands near your eyes or allow them to touch your lips. To avoid discomfort and burning, you might like to wear gloves. Chillies are also available minced in jars from supermarkets.*

Serves 6

ingredients

750g/1¹/₂lb rump steak, cut into strips
2 cloves garlic, crushed
1 tablespoon finely grated fresh ginger
1 tablespoon Thai Red Curry Paste
1 tablespoon sesame oil
1 tablespoon vegetable oil
1 onion, cut into wedges
1 green capsicum (pepper), chopped
1 red capsicum(pepper), chopped
440g/14oz canned baby sweet corn, drained
220g/7oz canned bamboo shoots, drained
1 tablespoon Thai fish sauce (nam pla)
1 tablespoon brown sugar
¹/₂ cup/125ml/4fl oz beef stock

pork
and pineapple with basil

Method:

1 Place shallots, chillies, galangal or ginger, lime leaves, lemon grass, tamarind, 1 tablespoon lime juice, water, shrimp paste and dried shrimps in a food processor and process to make a thick paste, adding a little more water if necessary.

2 Place pork in a bowl, add spice paste and toss to coat pork well.

3 Heat oil in a wok or large saucepan over a medium heat, add pork and stir-fry for 5 minutes or until fragrant and pork is just cooked.

4 Stir in sugar, coconut cream and milk and fish sauce and simmer, uncovered, for 8-10 minutes or until pork is tender.

5 Add pineapple and remaining lime juice and simmer for 3 minutes or until pineapple is heated. Stir in basil.

Serves 4

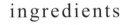

ingredients

4 red or golden shallots, chopped
2 fresh red chillies, finely chopped
3 cm/1¼in piece fresh galangal or ginger, finely chopped, or 5 slices bottled galangal, chopped
4 kaffir lime leaves
1 stalk fresh lemon grass, tender white part only, finely sliced, or
½ teaspoon dried lemon grass, soaked in hot water until soft
1 tablespoon tamarind concentrate
2 tablespoons lime juice
1 tablespoon water
2 teaspoons shrimp paste
1 tablespoon dried shrimps
350g/11oz pork fillets, cut into 3cm/1¼in cubes
1 tablespoon vegetable oil
1 teaspoon palm or brown sugar
1½ cups/375mL/12fl oz coconut cream
½ cup/125mL/4fl oz coconut milk
2 tablespoons Thai fish sauce (nam pla)
½ small (about 200g/6½oz) fresh pineapple, cut into 2cm/¾in wide strips
60g/2oz fresh basil leaves

exotic
tastes

beef
and bean stirfry

Method:

1 *Heat oil and garlic together in a wok over a medium heat, increase heat to high, add beef and stir-fry for 3 minutes or until beef changes colour.*

2 *Add beans, lime leaves, sugar and soy and fish sauces and stir-fry for 2 minutes or until beans change colour. Stir in coriander and serve immediately.*

Note: *Kaffir limes are a popular Thai ingredient. Both the fruit and the leaves have a distinctive flavour and perfume and are used in cooking. The leaves are available dried, fresh frozen or fresh from Oriental food shops and some greengrocers. If kaffir lime leaves are unavailable a little finely grated lime rind can be used instead.*

Serves 4

ingredients

2 teaspoons vegetable oil
2 cloves garlic, crushed
500g/1 lb topside or round steak,
cut into thin strips
185g/6oz snake (yard-long) or green beans,
cut into 10cm/4in lengths
2 kaffir lime leaves, shredded
2 teaspoons brown sugar
2 tablespoons light soy sauce
1 tablespoon Thai fish sauce (nam pla)
2 tablespoons coriander leaves

lamb
in mint

Method:

1 Cut eggplant (aubergine) into bite-sized chunks, place in a colander ad sprinkle with salt, mix well and leave to drain for 20 minutes. Rinse under cold water and drain well.

2 Heat oil in a wok or large frying pan. Add lamb and garlic and fry until well browned (you may need to do this in batches). Add eggplant (aubergine) and chilli and stirfry over a moderate heat for 5 minutes.

3 Stir in fish sauce, brown sugar, water and mint leaves and fry for a further 1 minute or until eggplant (aubergine) is softened. If sauce becomes too thick, add a little extra water. Serve with steamed long-grain rice.

Serves 4

ingredients

1 medium eggplant (aubergine)
1 tablespoon salt
2 tablespoons oil
500g/1lb lean lamb, thinly sliced
2 cloves garlic, chopped
1 red chilli, seeded and chopped
2 tablespoons brown sugar, well packed
1/3 cup 80ml/2½fl oz water
20 fresh mint leaves

muslin
beef curry

1 Place curry paste, shrimp paste, coconut milk, fish sauce, sugar, beef, peanuts, cinnamon and cardamom into a large saucepan and mix to combine. Bring to simmering over a medium heat, then simmer, stirring occasionally, uncovered, for 40 minutes or until beef is tender.

2 Stir in tamarind mixture and cook for 5 minutes longer. Remove cinnamon sticks and cardamom pods before serving.
Serves 4

ingredients

2 tablespoons Mussaman Curry Paste
¹/₂ teaspoon shrimp paste
2 cups/500mL/16fl oz coconut milk
1 tablespoon Thai fish sauce (nam pla)
1 tablespoon sugar
500g/1 lb rump steak, cut into
2cm/³/₄in cubes
155g/5oz peanuts, roasted
2 cinnamon sticks
5 cardamom pods
2 teaspoons tamarind concentrate,
dissolved in 2 tablespoons hot water

coconut
beef curry

Method:

1 Heat oil in a wok over a medium heat, add curry paste and stir-fry for 3 minutes or until fragrant. Add beef to pan and stir-fry for 5 minutes longer or until beef is brown.

2 Stir coconut milk into pan and bring to the boil. Reduce heat and simmer, stirring occasionally, for 15 minutes. Add zucchini (courgettes), red pepper (capsicum), tomatoes and spring onions and cook for 10 minutes longer or until beef is tender. Stir in basil leaves and serve.

Serves 4

ingredients

1 tablespoon vegetable oil
1 tablespoon Thai Red Curry
500 g/1 lb rump steak, thinly sliced
1¹/₂ cups/375mL/12fl oz coconut milk
2 zucchini (courgettes), sliced
1 red pepper (capsicum), chopped
125g/4oz cherry tomatoes
4 spring onions, sliced diagonally
12 fresh basil leaves

Cooking is not an exact science: one does not require finely calibrated scales, pipettes and scientific equipment to cook, yet the conversion to metric measures in some countries and its interpretations must have intimidated many a good cook.

Weights are given in the recipes only for ingredients such as meats, fish, poultry and some vegetables. Though a few grams/ounces one way or another will not affect the success of your dish.

Though recipes have been tested using the Australian Standard 250mL cup, 20mL tablespoon and 5mL teaspoon, they will work just as well with the US and Canadian 8fl oz cup, or the UK 300mL cup. We have used graduated cup measures in preference to tablespoon measures so that proportions are always the same. Where tablespoon measures have been given, these are not crucial measures, so using the smaller tablespoon of the US or UK will not affect the recipe's success. At least we all agree on the teaspoon size.

For breads, cakes and pastries, the only area which might cause concern is where eggs are used, as proportions will then vary. If working with a 250mL or 300mL cup, use large eggs (60g/2oz), adding a little more liquid to the recipe for 300mL cup measures if it seems necessary. Use the medium-sized eggs (55g/1¼oz) with 8fl oz cup measure. A graduated set of measuring cups and spoons is recommended, the cups in particular for measuring dry ingredients. Remember to level such ingredients to ensure their accuracy.

English measures

All measurements are similar to Australian with two exceptions: the English cup measures 300mL/10fl oz, whereas the Australian cup measure 250mL/8fl oz. The English tablespoon (the Australian dessertspoon) measures 14.8mL/½fl oz against the Australian tablespoon of 20mL/¾fl oz.

American measures

The American reputed pint is 16fl oz, a quart is equal to 32fl oz and the American gallon, 128fl oz. The Imperial measurement is 20fl oz to the pint, 40fl oz a quart and 160fl oz one gallon.

The American tablespoon is equal to 14.8mL/½fl oz, the teaspoon is 5mL/⅙fl oz. The cup measure is 250mL/8fl oz, the same as Australia.

Dry measures

All the measures are level, so when you have filled a cup or spoon, level it off with the edge of a knife. The scale below is the "cook's equivalent"; it is not an exact conversion of metric to imperial measurement. To calculate the exact metric equivalent yourself, use 2.2046 lb = 1kg or 1 lb = 0.45359kg

Metric		Imperial	
g = grams		oz = ounces	
kg = kilograms		lb = pound	
15g		½oz	
20g		⅔oz	
30g		1oz	
60g		2oz	
90g		3oz	
125g		4oz	¼ lb
155g		5oz	
185g		6oz	
220g		7oz	
250g		8oz	½ lb
280g		9oz	
315g		10oz	
345g		11oz	
375g		12oz	¾ lb
410g		13oz	
440g		14oz	
470g		15oz	
1,000g	1kg	35.2oz	2.2 lb
	1.5kg		3.3 lb

Oven temperatures

The Celsius temperatures given here are not exact; they have been rounded off and are given as a guide only. Follow the manufacturer's temperature guide, relating it to oven description given in the recipe. Remember gas ovens are hottest at the top, electric ovens at the bottom and convection-fan forced ovens are usually even throughout. We included Regulo numbers for gas cookers which may assist. To convert °C to °F multiply °C by 9 and divide by 5 then add 32.

Oven temperatures

	C°	F°	Regulo
Very slow	120	250	1
Slow	150	300	2
Moderately slow	160	325	3
Moderate	180	350	4
Moderately hot	190-200	370-400	5-6
Hot	210-220	410-440	6-7
Very hot	230	450	8
Super hot	250-290	475-500	9-10

Cake dish sizes

Metric	Imperial
15cm	6in
18cm	7in
20cm	8in
23cm	9in

Loaf dish sizes

Metric	Imperial
23x12cm	9x5in
25x8cm	10x3in
28x18cm	11x7in

Liquid measures

Metric	Imperial	Cup & Spoon
mL	fl oz	
millilitres	fluid ounce	
5mL	1/6fl oz	1 teaspoon
20mL	2/3fl oz	1 tablespoon
30mL	1fl oz	1 tablespoon plus 2 teaspoons
60mL	2fl oz	1/4 cup
85mL	2 1/2fl oz	1/3 cup
100mL	3fl oz	3/8 cup
125mL	4fl oz	1/2 cup
150mL	5fl oz	1/4 pint, 1 gill
250mL	8fl oz	1 cup
300mL	10fl oz	1/2 pint)
360mL	12fl oz	1 1/2 cups
420mL	14fl oz	1 3/4 cups
500mL	16fl oz	2 cups
600mL	20fl oz 1 pint,	2 1/2 cups
1 litre	35fl oz 1 3/4 pints,	4 cups

Cup measurements

One cup is equal to the following weights.

	Metric	Imperial
Almonds, flaked	90g	3oz
Almonds, slivered, ground	125g	4oz
Almonds, kernel	155g	5oz
Apples, dried, chopped	125g	4oz
Apricots, dried, chopped	190g	6oz
Breadcrumbs, packet	125g	4oz
Breadcrumbs, soft	60g	2oz
Cheese, grated	125g	4oz
Choc bits	155g	5oz
Coconut, desiccated	90g	3oz
Cornflakes	30g	1oz
Currants	155g	5oz
Flour	125g	4oz
Fruit, dried (mixed, sultanas etc)	185g	6oz
Ginger, crystallised, glace	250g	8oz
Honey, treacle, golden syrup	315g	10oz
Mixed peel	220g	7oz
Nuts, chopped	125g	4oz
Prunes, chopped	220g	7oz
Rice, cooked	155g	5oz
Rice, uncooked	220g	7oz
Rolled oats	90g	3oz
Sesame seeds	125g	4oz
Shortening (butter, margarine)	250g	8oz
Sugar, brown	155g	5oz
Sugar, granulated or caster	250g	8oz
Sugar, sifted icing	155g	5oz
Wheatgerm	60g	2oz

Length

Some of us still have trouble converting imperial length to metric. In this scale, measures have been rounded off to the easiest-to-use and most acceptable figures.

To obtain the exact metric equivalent in converting inches to centimetres, multiply inches by 2.54 whereby 1 inch equals 25.4 millimetres and 1 millimetre equals 0.03937 inches.

Metric	Imperial
mm=millimetres	in = inches
cm=centimetres	ft = feet
5mm, 0.5cm	1/4in
10mm, 1.0cm	1/2in
20mm, 2.0cm	3/4in
2.5cm	1in
5cm	2in
8cm	3in
10cm	4in
12cm	5in
15cm	6in
18cm	7in
20cm	8in
23cm	9in
25cm	10in
28cm	11in
30cm	1 ft, 12in